Pretty Lies and Ocean Eyes

By Mia Carter

Thank you to every person who has supported me in any way, without you, none of this would have ever been possible and I am eternally grateful.

Here lies a book

Of things I couldn't bare

To speak aloud

These words that crawl around

In the seams of my heart and mind

Have managed to find themselves

Scattered across these simple pages

Spilling all of my deepest hidden feelings

Begging for someone

Just anyone to relate to

Each copy holds a small fragment

Of my bare and vulnerable soul

And here I sit

Willingly gifting it to you

(Do with it what you will)

Fragile heart

How many times

Must you completely shatter

Before you realize

The truth has always been

Right in front of our eyes

We can debate

Whether something is half full

Or half empty all day

But either way

Half of my heart is gone

And whether it is

Half full

Or half empty

Is completely irrelevant

(It hurts the same)

Don't concern yourself with the color

Ocean eyes are just eyes

That are so alluring

You would drown

Without a fight

Just to get your feet wet

In the depths of their mind

"You're early, again

Why can't you just stay away

I told you the last time

You summoned me here

You'll eventually be mine

But, Mi Amor, today is not that day

You still have our entire life to live"

(Death speaks with love, I can't help but call Him back)

You've been battling with yourself

For so many years

But you only see the pain left over

You don't see

That every scar that you left

Every cruel word you've spoken

Every time you intentionally hurt yourself

Has only made you bulletproof

You're so much stronger now

(And I'm so proud of you)

My love for you

Is written in the stars

Just like the moon

Reaches for the tide

Pulling it home

My heart is drawn to yours

As long as the sun rises

You have a place in my soul

A simple promise

That lingers on my tongue

It has been etched in stone

And Father Time refuses to touch it

(You're my constant when everything is chaotic)

I've always loved magic

So don't be surprised

When my final act

Is disappearing

Don't worry my love

I'll leave a dozen sunflowers

And a book to hold my place

(Did you really expect me to leave you with nothing?)

You found a home

In my ribcage

Knowing I would protect you

From the world

And knowing

I could never turn you away

The only thing I am asking of you

Is to please stay

Being with you

Is like doing cartwheels

On a tightrope

Trying to balance

My heart and my mind

I know falling will kill me

There is no safety net to catch me

There is no soft landing below

But still here I am

Bouncing on the rope

Bracing for impact

But still praying

I'll learn to fly

Before I hit the ground

Before a star collapses

It will glow the brightest

It ever has

That is my only thought

When I see

Your celestial smile

Putting the sun to shame

(Please don't burn out)

You fought every dragon

Who guarded my heart

Little did I know

The reason you defeated them all

So effortlessly

Is because

You too are a dragon

The only difference is

You are so much more ferocious

Than the gentle giants

Who called my heart a home

When you hold him at night

Make sure you're gentle

He is more broken than he will ever admit

His heart has been shattered

To what he sees as beyond repair

So please be patient

Give him all the time he needs

Be the glue that holds him together

No matter how small and jagged the pieces may be

Just please be gentle with him

He has been through more than enough

They say to fall in love with a writer

It's the only way to never die

But what happens

When you follow that advice

And fall in love with the writer

Who isn't in love with you

You're left with one sided notebooks

Filled with tears and half-finished poems

And a crack in your heart

Filled with words they wrote

Just never about you

That's her gift

She draws you in with innocent eyes

And a voice that drips like honey

She'll steal your heart right off your sleeve

And you won't realize

She was ever that close

Until she finally leaves

And you're left feeling empty

A permanent reflection

Of flames dance in my eyes

Don't look for too long

They might burn you too

(You're something I refuse to destroy)

You were water

Too peaceful to disturb

While I was the fire

Blazing too wildly to control

Realizing far too late

All it would take is once touch to

Douse my flames

And send me up in smoke

I could compare him to the sun

You'd understand

If you saw

The way the light kisses

Everything surrounding him

Maybe the moon is a better fit for him

He only shows his face

When all the other light has left

And I am drawn to him

Like a wolf awaits the moon

Green eyes

Red lips

Black soul

Golden heart

(Colors of my life)

Tell me you love me

Lie to me

If you have to

I just need to feel

Wanted by you

Make me feel like

I'm the queen of your world

Even if I'm not

I'll still show you

How it feels

To be the king of mine

She left a trail

Of cigarette butts

Behind her

The ends covered

In her signature

Bright red lipstick

It's her way of saying goodbye

And at the same time

Begging you to follow her

You say

When I'm laying with you

My hair looks like a golden halo

I tried to warn you

The halo is only there

To hide my horns

The Devil was an angel too

I'll only destroy you

If you put your faith in me

I collect my flaws

As if they are the most valuable

Thing I own

Placing them all front and center

Destroying any and all

Self esteem

That has crawled inside my mind

I recite all the things wrong with me

As if I'm quoting scriptures

Like that is the only truth I know

But I am wrong

It took me 21 years

To finally see

My flaws make me unique

They are what make me

My own type of beautiful

And even on the days

When I cannot see it

I am still enough

(I was always enough)

Her hair frames her face in waves

Her eyes pull you in like the tide

Poetry spills from her coral colored lips like water

And freckles scatter across her skin like grains of sand

Her touch is gentle like the waves

You could never imagine

The power that radiates just beneath the surface

(She is the sea personified)

I may seem like an open book

Begging to be read

Enticing you with daring tales of adventure

But darling

All my secrets are written in Latin

And you don't care enough to translate

(Latin is a dead language and it took my secrets to the grave with it)

They say smoke follows beauty

And now I finally understand

Why the smoke swirls around your head

Forming a hazy halo

With every drag of your cigarette

I had a dream I was karma

With the full ability

To give you everything you deserve

But I still couldn't bring myself

To hurt you in any way

Knowing that if the tables were turned

You wouldn't hesitate

To wreak havoc on my life

(Our hearts were never the same)

Endings are never truly beautiful

So I take the words

That best describe the pain I feel

And warp them

Into a narrative that is beautiful

I speak of this emptiness as the ocean

The stars have become beacons in the night

Every object has become some poetic thing

When in reality

There is nothing beautiful about

The pain in my chest

These broken screams

Leaving my mouth

Are petrifying

(The sounds of heartbreak are not poetic)

When I told you

That you are the only person

I would willingly let

Break my heart

I really hoped you wouldn't

Treat it as a challenge

I can't help wonder

If my face flashes through your mind

When you read poetry

Even if only for a brief second

(Do you ever think of me?)

You buried your feelings

So deep

That no matter how much

I dug

And no matter how hard

I tried

I could never reach them

She left a crater so large

I could never fill that space

Yet still I tried

I tried to show you

Not all green eyed girls

Will shatter your heart

But no matter what I try

She still occupies the space

Where your heart should be

Here I stand

Shovel in hand

Walking into the woods

To uncover the sadness

I buried among the wilderness

(One day dead things will stop calling me back)

She's a siren

Luring men to their deaths

Singing softly enough

To captivate their minds

Just long enough

To send them crashing

Her beauty

Subtle yet enchanting

Bringing the strongest of men

To their knees

But you

You were able to resist

Her siren call

You were able to get away

Now she's lost

Wondering what went wrong

She's resentful now

Patiently waiting in the dark

To lure some

Unknown man

Into the rocks

Hoping that one day

You'll remember her

And come back to her

Oh (sweetheart)

As much as you wish you could

You can't blame him

(He) isn't the one who (broke) you

He warned you from the start

You would never have a place

In his heart

You exaggerated his feelings for you

You lived in a land of make believe

Believing that he actually saw you

As anything more than

A distraction to constantly feed his ego

Believe (me) sweet girl

When I say

I wish I could take away the pain

But it's something only you can heal

I learned that the hard way (too)

You continuously grasp my hands

Seeking the roses

That dangle between my fingers

Only to recoil

When you clutch the thorns

That have embedded themselves

Deeply inside of my palms

(I'm so sorry, love. I didn't mean to hurt you)

I told the moon our story

Recited every last minuscule detail

Under her comforting glow

And I guess the clouds were listening too

It has been raining since that night

Without showing the slightest sign

Of slowing down

Sweetheart I warned you about loving me

I don't know how to stay

I told you

You would continually have to pull the jagged edges of my soul

Out of your hands for months after I leave

When you told me you were afraid of ghosts

I begged you to run

I think we both knew

It was too late to save you

At that point it became inevitable

I would haunt every inch of your mind

Whispering your name

Every night you spend alone

No amount of prayers and exorcisms

Could save you from the ghost I left residing in you

No amount of cleaning

Could really pick up every broken shard that I left you in

I'm sorry love

I really am

Why did you not just run when you had the chance?

He has cigarette eyes

Lighting up the night

If you look a little closer

At the glowing embers

You'll notice

He is about to burn out

You see the danger in my eyes

I feel the safety in your firm embrace

The death-grip you wrap me in

Soothes my soul to the deepest part

My dependence on feeling your calm

Balances my wild

I'm sorry love

I hope you understand why I had to leave

My dreams are far too big

To be confined to this one town

Small town lights

Are drowning out what I could be

So please

Don't take it personally when I disappear

I'll leave my heart with you though

Just so you know

You'll always have a part of me

(Take care of it please)

Like a dandelion

Pieces of her scatter in the wind

Granting wishes and keeping secrets

You never know when you'll find her

All you know is

When you need her

She is right there

Ready to grant any wish

And then vanish into thin air

She's a dandelion

Born to be free

Born to prove that wishes still come true

You just have to believe

My mind was a nuclear war zone

Traces of utter destruction

Lingered on every thought

Until I met you

Suddenly

Flowers began to bloom

In fields that were once barren

And brimming with radiation

Butterflies appeared again

Rainbow wings flutter along

To the enchanting melody of your voice

The water is clear now

And a vibrant blue has replaced

The murky brown water

That I was certain

I would drown in

She is a lighthouse on the coast

A lantern for the lonely

She is a breath of fresh air

When you're drowning

She is a shoulder to cry on

And a home cooked meal

She is all things comforting

Do you think

She is an angel

Doomed to spend a lifetime on Earth

(She still has her wings please don't break them)

All I do is jump

Straight into his arms

The moment he calls

Without fail

As if I have already forgotten

The last time he let me fall

For you

I try and hide my wings

In fear you'll clip them

Hoping maybe if you didn't see them

You wouldn't break them

But you're the Devil

Hiding behind pretty eyes

Waiting for the perfect opportunity

To destroy the biggest part of me

(An angel can't expect to keep her wings if she resides in Hell)

I didn't mind

Giving him pieces of me

So he could mend

All the broken parts inside him

Until he took my pieces

That I ripped from my soul

And gave them to her

I'm standing on broken glass

Begging for your hand

To pull me out of this hell

Instead

You pushed me down

And laughed

At how weak

I have become

(I was so strong before you)

Sweet girl

You exhausted all of your energy

Saving everyone else

That you didn't realize

You too were sinking

Faster than anyone you brought back to the surface

Now you're drowning

And no matter how hard you kick

You can't seem to keep your head above water

And the saddest part of it all

Is that I know he could have loved me

But he met her first

And I'm only second best

She has his heart

While I have his 3AM poetry

And

Every broken piece

She left him in

Right in front of me

While he begs me to fix his heart

Only to never hold it

What will become of my soul when I die?

Will I wander the Earth

Forever left in purgatory

Saint Peter told me I can't enter the gates

God himself said it's too late to save my soul

The hell hounds snarl and snap

Not letting me near the gates of hell either

Satan said he has no use for a soul that belongs to someone else

All because you stole my soul

Before God could save it

Or the Devil imprison it

I'm doomed to purgatory

For all of eternity

All because of you

Darling your touch was like Midas

My skin turned golden with every touch

Until your fingertips

Starting leaving trails of corrosion

Tarnishing my gilded body

You ruined me

Truth be told

Even knowing what I would become

I would still gladly be destroyed by you

Over and over again

The sea is calling to me again

But this time

It's not a gentle whisper

Luring me back to the shore

She is angry and demanding this time

Questioning why I have been away so long

She screams at me

Blaming me for all the sailors she's brought home

And for every ship capsized

While she is trying to fill the hole I left

Don't worry my love

I'll be home soon

Everything will be alright

You thought you would break me

When you cut my wings

But you forgot

I still have claws like a tiger

And my teeth are like razors

I promise one day

I will make you feel

The exact pain

I'm living in

At this moment

I hope that

Where your heart

Led you

Made you happy

I hope that

Where your heart

Led you

Made you free

I hope that

You're happy

Even though it was

Without me

Everything you sing

Is my favorite song

You give me that front row feeling

With every verse

Hummed just for me

She is not scared of spiders

Or snakes

Or monsters

Or the dark

Or heights

The things that scare her

Should bring her comfort

Attachment scares her

Feelings scare her

People scare her

Love is paralyzing

The thought that you

Might care about her

Is electrifying

But absolutely terrifying

Everyone called her a doll

From the time she was a child

It wasn't until she was older

That she realized

How true everyone was

She is still thrown around

Played with and then put up

Easily forgotten

Whenever something new comes

Patiently for someone to remember her

And want to hold her again

I have constellations

In my bones

And an entire galaxy

Hand painted on my soul

Moonlight courses through my veins

I watch the skies with determined longing in my eyes

I am always wishing for a home

Far away from Earth

Can't you see?

I am made of stardust and comets

I am meant to soar among the planets

Earth is only temporary for me

When I finally disappear

Don't grieve for me

Just know I am finally home

Living among the stars

Sleeping on the moon

Riding the comets like roller coasters

Skating around Saturn's rings

If you pay close attention

You'll see me again

Waving to Earth from a shooting star

On a night when you think you're all alone

So make a wish and smile

Smile knowing I'm finally home

I would rather have a flower crown

Made of daffodils and daisies

Than a bullshit tiara

Decorated with fake jewels

(My crown doesn't determine my worth)

I am a storm

A whirlwind of chaos

But even the strongest of storms

Have to break

     And break

        And break

You know how the story goes

Once upon a time

A handsome prince

Wooed the princess

Reciting intricate promises

And intoxicating compliments

But this story has a twist

He was slaying every dragon

For a queen in a land

Far far away from the princess's home

Leaving the princess to fend for herself

The princess soon became queen

And she made sure

To build the walls of her kingdom

So high

That no creature

Nor any human could enter

She grew the reputation of a savage

But how can they blame her

The prince stole her heart

And from that day forward

She vowed to protect herself at all costs

(Even the most malicious dragons refuse to speak her name)

What I once thought

Were butterflies in my stomach

Turned out to be

Moths

Who only needed somewhere

Empty to hide

Until something brighter

Came along

Now even the moths are gone

(They left with you)

You know I've always been drawn to danger

There's a fire dancing in your eyes

Waiting to be set free

I'll willingly let the blaze consume

Every last fiber of my being

But you want to keep the flames contained

And I don't blame you

Once you've been burned

You'll do whatever you can

To protect yourself

From feeling that pain again

(I still believe you're worth burning for)

You stubbornly promise that you don't love her

But the idea of her flirting

With another man

Is enough to make you green with envy

You adamantly swear you don't love her

But the sight of her in tears

Is all it takes to break down your tough exterior

You relentlessly insist that you don't love her

But the mention of her disappearing

Is an absolutely terrifying concept

You vehemently vow that you don't love her

But it's okay

Your secret is safe with her

As far as anyone knows

She doesn't love you either

(Secrets)

There's something different about her

You can't exactly tell what it is

But if you ask

Children will tell you

That she was a mermaid ruling the ocean

Commanding the waves to dance for her

But she was dragged from her home

Kicking and screaming to a concrete jungle

With no ocean in sight

Instead of the soft lullaby

Of the tide crashing against the shore

She only hears cars colliding

Her voice that lured men to her

Is now raspy and broken

But listen closely

When it rains

You can see her

Sitting outside watching the sky

Softly singing as the raindrops

Leave trails of kisses on her skin

It's almost as if

The water misses her too

He's a terrible habit

That I'm not sure

I want to quit

He's killing me

But I've never felt so alive

So I breathe him in

(Just one more time)

He found me

At a time

When the dust of my destruction

Was still floating in the air around me

But without hesitation

He fearlessly reached

Into the smoldering rubble

In an attempt to save me

Before I completely self-imploded

(I could never thank him enough)

I swear

I don't care

But this empty feeling

Seeping from my chest

Shows me

How much of a lie

I'm telling myself

(Rejection)

You only come to me

When your cup has become empty

Without fail every time you return

I give you all I have

(You drained me and had the audacity to blame me for having nothing

left to give)

You reminded me of the life I used to have

Before my wings deteriorated in front of my eyes

Long before I memorized the smell of charred feathers

The horrid stench lingers

Haunting the air of my dreams

I tried to grasp onto the comets

Just to slow my descent to this hell

Only to char my palms on their tails

As a last futile attempt to save myself

From spending a lifetime on Earth

I tried to hold onto the sun

Maybe that's where my skin picked up this new glow

I still long for the days

When I didn't have little scorch marked freckles

Scattered across my body

As a subtle reminder of my descent

The only blessing that came

From losing my wings

(Along with my mind)

Is that without falling from grace

I would have never met you

And you're as close to heaven

As I'll ever be again

If you couldn't be bothered to love her now

You can't choose to just

Come back and love her later

Even ancient buildings that have stood resiliently

Against the sands of time

Tremble when you speak

It's no surprise that you brought me to my knees

(I never stood a chance)

I used to think

The world was black and white

With an occasional grey area

Until you opened my eyes

To see the rainbow of colors

That is my life

Right in front of me

(Has the sky always been this blue?)

I believe in aliens

And Bigfoot

I believe in God

I believe in leprechauns

And fairies

Even mermaids

So many mythical creatures

So much complete and utter nonsense

I don't understand

Why is it so damn hard for me to believe

That someone might actually care about me

They judge you by your scars

They judge you by your dark clothing

And frizzy hair

They don't see

The kaleidoscope of color

Hiding in your eyes

Or the kindness you show

To every passing stranger

They only see what they want

But don't worry about them

I see you for you

And you are more than enough

You're the ocean

And I'm drowning in your depths

I wish you could see

Nothing else on Earth

Could ever compare to you

There are days when

I truly believe I hate you

But then it occurs to me

Without you

I would have never found my strength

Or found the beauty in my flaws

I wouldn't know what it felt like to be

Truly happy

In all honesty

It's no secret

I could never hate you

(Because I'll always love you)

You'll think of her

It may not be today

Or tomorrow

Or even this year

But one day

Her memory will hit you like a hurricane

You'll remember her shaky voice

When she sang for you

For the first time

You'll catch the smell of her perfume

In a crowded room

And frantically search for her face

Within the sea of strangers

You'll relive every fleeting moment

Whenever someone mentions the one who got away

You'll think of her

And I hope it kills you inside

Knowing that she would have done anything

To make you stay with her

Today it may feel

As if the world is against you

But darling

That doesn't change what you're made of

I know it all seems utterly impossible

But please remember

A sunflower will always be a sunflower

Even in the moonlight

She doesn't know how to find the evil in people

She looks the devil in the eyes

And doesn't flinch or cower

If you ask her why

She'll simply explain

That he's misunderstood

And no one has given him a chance

To tell his side of the story

Maybe that's her problem

She's too blinded by her own naivety

To see that not all people have the same heart as her

She is an angel walking among the living

(Someone protect her or this world will break her)

Your eyes scream of danger

They taunt me with promises of adventure

And the reckless fool that I am

Refuses to stay away

I'm drawn to you

Like a moth to a flame

You tell me I'm changing

But I feel exactly the same

Did I give away too many pieces?

Am I too empty now?

Is it showing on the outside too?

(I say I feel the same, but I never felt this empty before)

You call me trouble

And I say you're a mess

We're too busy

Comparing flaws

To see

That we are one in the same

Looking at each other

In the mirror

(Baby I am summertime)

I am sunshine on your tanned skin

And a gentle breeze

Blowing through your hair

I'm not cold

I'm not bitter

(But) you always take me for granted

Until I'm no longer here

(You only deserve the winter months)

She speaks in poems

As sunlight softly kisses her hair

The wind carries her

From place to place

As water dances for her

Her eyes hold flames

That scream of mischief

She's much more than she believes she is

If only she could see

What everyone else sees in her

He jokingly told me

I should have came with a warning label

After all

Every addictive thing has one

(I'll never tell him, but he needs one too)

I read somewhere that

Silly little crushes

Inspire art

So spectacular

That museums all over the world

Would fight for a chance

To showcase it

Even if only for a few hours

(A muse like him, belongs next to the Mona Lisa)

I have no doubt

When it comes to that man

He could change the world

If he truly wanted to

Into something completely unrecognizable

After all

All it took was a playful smirk

For my world

To be flipped upside down

And when it comes to you

One step forward

Will always be

At least

Seven steps backward

(You refuse to let me keep up no matter how hard I try)

When I was younger

I didn't seem to understand

Exactly why my mother

Broke that CD into a million pieces

And threw it out the window

Until I had my heart broken

And that song you used to sing to me

Played through the speakers of my car

(There's a shattered CD on the side of the interstate with your name

written on it)

You tease me

For my short attention span

But sweetheart

That doesn't apply to you

I have memorized everything

Insignificant thing you have ever told me

I'm sorry

Nothing on this planet

Could hold my attention

Whenever you're speaking

(You have to be magic)

I'm trying to learn to love myself again

But it feels like I'm drowning

The waves grow higher

And I don't want to hold my breath

So I let the salt water

Fill my lungs

While the water recites whispers

Of every harsh word ever spoken against me

I wanted to learn

Everything about your love language

But all we seem to do

Is speak in tongues

Never understanding

The foreign words

That I so desperately

Wish to decipher

I laugh and say

He's just a crush

But he has inspired

More of my poetry

Than the oceans and stars

Even if he is only a fantasy

That I will never obtain

When I write

He is mine

And that is something

I can hold on to

You crawled your way

Into my dreams last night

I guess

You dug your claws

So deep into my mind

That even my subconscious

Is immersed with thoughts of you

(Stay out of my dreams, I think of you enough when I'm awake)

I always searched for tranquility

Only to find continuous chaos

Shattering the walls of my sanity

I thrive in the wake of devastation

And dance in the ashes of destruction

How can you ever expect

To find the calm aftermath

Without first surviving the storms

You threw my heart on the floor

Without so much as a second thought

Not even bothering a half-hearted apology

As a feeble attempt to soften the blow

Now here I am

With blood up to my elbows

And nails stained red

Trying to fit the pieces of my heart together again

Just so I can remember what it is like

To have a regular heartbeat

(Shattered hearts don't feel the same)

I had grown accustomed to the cold storm

Residing inside of my bones

Until he came along

And now no amount of rain

Can douse the fire

He ignited in my soul

(Please don't let me burn out)

Poetry gracefully rolls off his tongue

Almost as if

I am the only muse

He has ever known

His demanding lips

Caress my skin

Painting my body

With different hues

Of purple and blue

His gentle hands

Trace every scar

Every slight imperfection

While he shows me

Just how perfect

He believes that I am

In a way only he can

I wondered if you ever looked for me

So many times

I told you exactly where I would run

When everything around us went south

If you ever find yourself

Where the land meets the sea

Look for my footprints in the sand

And overturn every fallen palm leaf

Maybe just maybe

You'll find me again

Exactly where I am meant to be

(You should have known I'd be here)

I still remember

The night you teased me for my sweet tooth

Laughing and warning me that

All this sugar is only going to rot my teeth

I should have known

That all you would ever do

Is continually feed me

Sugar coated lies

And sweet empty promises

But my teeth never changed

Instead all of your sweet lies

Decayed my soul from the inside out

I'm too reckless

To handle someone

So precious

(Why don't you run from me love? I'm going to break you)

You can blame me if you want

Tell everyone that I never fought for you

But how was I supposed

To fight for you

When you were the one

Fighting me

She has the entire bar mesmerized

With a beer in one hand and a microphone in the other

Anyone could see

She's a hell bound angel

A whiskey bent

Heart break in heels

Chasing you

Like a shot

Of my favorite whiskey

Everything I want to say

Is burning my throat

Begging to be heard

So I keep drinking

Swallowing shot after shot

Drowning my pride

Suffocating every unsaid thought

With just one more shot

You lit a fire in my bones

The flames grow higher

With every touch

Scorching my soul

Just to keep you warm

From the bitter cold of sleeping alone

You won't stay long

You'll find a brighter fire

And leave me burning

An empty shell with embers for eyes

Your name forever dancing in my flames

Tangled in sandy sheets

Nothing but skin on skin

Leaving me with

One last lingering kiss

Knowing we will never speak again

Don't ask why

She acts so cold

Toward you now

She burned herself out

Keeping you warm

And she would rather

Be damned

Than to give anyone

That power again

Like sand in an hourglass

Our time is running out

Slow and steady

I can see you pulling away

So I tried to flip us back over

Attempting to salvage what I know I'm losing

But the sand only flowed faster to the bottom

We just ran out of time

And now I'm left as empty

As the top of the hourglass

She's not enough for you now

Or maybe she is too much

But one day

You're going to realize

She was everything you needed

She didn't care about the material possessions

She only wanted you

She would have given up her dreams for you

She worshiped the ground you walked on

But you let her go

Simply because she was too much

Or was it not enough

You were too scared to let her in

But you'll remember her

Every time tequila touches your lips

You're going to wish you did more

To hold on to her

Dabbing my tears dry

Replacing every drop

With a new coat of mascara

Removing every trace

That it was once

Running down my face

Painting my lips

Cherry red

Trying to hide how I really feel

If I'm going to be a wreck

I'll make sure

You can't look away

If she really wanted to

With the snap of her fingers

She could make Lucifer himself

Get on his knees and pray to God

She is surrounded by his hell fire

But he would never

Let the flames scorch her

Playing Russian roulette

With every conversation

Will this one

Be the one that

Kills me

Or do I live to play another game

She doesn't see what you see in her

She notices every flaw

She picks herself apart

To the point of having nothing left

Every blemish

Every stretch mark

Every small imperfection

Is magnified in her eyes

She doesn't see

How her eyes light up

When she talks about the things she loves

She doesn't see

The constellations of freckles dancing across her body

She doesn't see

How she glows when the sun kisses her skin

She doesn't see

Anything you do have

So be patient with her

Remind her

Every chance you get

That she is beautiful

That she is more than enough for you

Remind her you care

And watch her

Bloom

Of course I love stereotypical compliments

About my looks and other superficial things

But if you want to truly flatter me

Tell me about how I make your life better

Since I've been in it

Softly whisper about how I make you feel alive

For the first time in years

Elaborate about how much you care for me

Confess that I actually mean something to you

Say that you love me

For so much more than what I do for you physically

Speak to my soul

(And please just tell the truth)

I strategically built this fortress

In a feeble attempt to protect

The remnants of my heart

Brick by brick

With intricately places thorns

Placed along each layer of cement

I thought I was safe here

The walls I built were impenetrable

But you destroyed

Everything I took so long to built

With one shift motion

The hardest part

About loving you

Was knowing

From the start

That I couldn't really hold you

I would have to let you go

And you would laugh

As you took my heart

Without ever looking back

You're not hard to love

On the contrary

You're far too easy to love

That's why they push you away

You make them fall too fast

And it is terrifying

I will always be the woman

To love monsters

And trust me I know

No matter how much I love every sharp fanged beast

And no matter how much the monsters love me

I will never change their nature

Just as they will never change mine

I wrote your name in stone

You wrote mine in the sand

I knew the tide

Would wash me away

And it wouldn't take long for you

To forget my face

While your name would eternally etched

A hauntingly beautiful

Reminder of what could have been

Somehow he has convinced himself

That he deserves to burn

And that could not be

Further from the truth

That man deserves

The stars

The moon

And even the sun

He deserves a love

As pure as snow

And gentle as the rain

If anyone deserves to burn

It is the woman

Who clouded his clear eyes

Keeping people at arm's length

Only lasts for so long

Eventually your resolve will falter

And they will find their way in

You might not even realize

How far they made it

Until you try to push them away again

And suddenly it feels as if they are pulling

Your heart and lungs along with them

While you push them away

It will hurt so much more than you imagined

One person breaking down the wall

Was all it took for you to see

Not everyone you let in wants destroy you

Some only want to make flowers grow

In the cracks others left

They aren't here to cause more pain

They only want to help rebuild your broken pieces

Only to craft them into something more magnificent

Than you've ever seen before

One day you'll see

Arm's length

Isn't as great as it seems

Your favorite flower was always a rose

I was always a wildflower

I do not blame you for that

Domesticated beauty has a level of elegance

I could never possess

But I will always prefer

The freedom of letting the wind decide my fate

I'll let you in on a secret

While roses wilt

The wildflowers always grow back

(No matter how many times it has been stomped on)

I will always be the woman

Who is fascinated with storms

You will always be able to find me

With my nose pressed against

A window

Watching the rain race down glass

Casting its own shadow on my face

Never losing my excitement with each stroke of lightning

The wind will always dance in my eyes

And even when the thunder makes me jump

I can't help but love

The chaos of the storm

How do you expect me to believe in fairytale love?

All I've ever seen is broken marriages

Broken homes

And cycles of abuse

Never have I seen two people stay together for better or worse

Vows of forever taken at the alter

Blown away with the wind

So before you ask

No I don't believe in happily ever after

But what I do believe in

Is us

I think we can make it work

Just two people against the world

Don't promise me forever

Just promise me we can try

Just because

I am the one

Who is writing

Doesn't change the fact

That you

Are still the ink

That bleeds from my pen

And leaves a stain

On each and every blank page

No matter how tough

She appears to be

To the outside world

Those that truly know her

Know that she

Is the most gentle soul

(She's just tired of being hurt)

Come slow dance with me

In the soft glow

Of dimmed headlights

On a dirt road

In the middle of nowhere

Nothing in sight

But rows of Alabama pines

The crickets are singing along

To the low hum of the radio

Just two people

Love drunk

In the moonlight

Wishing they could stay

Like this forever

Like the sun and moon

I continually chase you

Only to briefly touch

On the rare occasion of an eclipse

But to have you

Even if only for a few fleeting moments

Is enough to make me chase you until the end of time

Hades and Persephone

Will always be my favorite love story

It's not typical

Or ideal

But still

My favorite

You can't hide the light

That radiates from the depths of your soul

But be careful love

All that light

In such a dark place

Is bound to attract much more sinister things than moths

I heard our song today

I couldn't sing along like we used to

I'm not sure how I made it home

The last fifteen minutes

Were a blur

And I'm not sure if

It was the speed I was driving

Or the tears in my eyes

The salt that has been

Ruthlessly rubbed in my wounds

Still doesn't compare

To the burn inside of my chest

At the thought of your hands

On someone else's body

I know you're struggling

Fighting just to keep

Your head above the water

Your body is fighting

Against nature

I know you're tired

And we both know

My love is

Weighing you down

Cut the rope that is

Holding is together

(Let me drown and save yourself)

My body is painted

With the colors

Of your beautiful mess

I don't remember how

I looked before this

(I) warned you

About the storm brewing on the horizon

The waves inside my soul

Grew much too rough

Much too fast

Even though you promised to stay

And brace the storm with me

I knew you wouldn't

My love (was never enough)

Of a reason to risk yourself

But darling

You're passive

I'm simply aggressive

Of course we are bound to clash

Whether it is a bloody mess

Or you just let me go

The end is completely inevitable

Even though your hands touched my body

The fading marks you left

Will never compare

To the patterns his touch

Embedded in my soul

I have always given away

Pieces of my broken soul

To people who don't deserve me

It was too late

When I realized

I needed those pieces for myself

(I can't pour when my cup is empty)

His velvet voice

Always lying with ease

And yet I still listen

To every empty promise

That gracefully falls from his lips

I drink each lie like a fine wine

Until I'm intoxicated

With the idea

That maybe

This time

When he tells me he loves me

He will be telling the truth

Writing my book of lies

The first page is scribbled with your name

Above the words

"I don't love you"

I'll never admit the truth

Just like you won't admit

That you love me too

I write letters to you in the sand

People marvel at the lines of poetry

Decorating the shore

They tell me how lucky you must be

To have someone who writes only for you

But inevitably the moment I sign my name

The tide washes all of my words away

(Love letters you'll never see)

Eventually I had to come to terms

With the fact that

No matter how much love

I showered him with

He will always reek of heartbreak

And I will simply be collateral damage

In the battle

Brewing within his mind

After all this time

I am still trying to learn

How your pastel hands

Could possibly leave

Such vibrant neon patterns

On my skin

Why do you do cherry pick

The desirable parts of me

But discard who I actually am

You don't get to choose

Which parts of me that you

Deem worthy of your love

And utterly discard

Everything else I have to offer

You deserve the moon

And the stars

And someone who will love you

Without conditions

Or restrictions

You deserve the purest love

You deserve a happiness

That will make you forget

About the person who

Destroyed your heart

And made you afraid to feel

Anything for anyone again

You will never hear me utter

Those three little words

But deep down

I know in my heart

That the regret that will wrack my body

For never admitting how I feel

Won't compare to the pain

Of you not being able

To say you love me too

You're heaven

I'm hell

You're streets of gold

And an eternity of peace

While I smell of sulfur

And will only bring you suffering

Don't burn yourself

On my flames

Trying to save me

(I won't let hellfire scorch him)

I let you go

But you never left

You still crawl your way

Out of my pen

Preserving your face

On every line of poetry

Your voice echoes my own

Reciting lines of heartbreak

And staining my words

As much as I want to get rid of you

Without you

My writing disappears too

You chased me to the edge

Daring me to fall

Knowing

When I hit the ground

You'll be long gone

Moved on to prettier things

And I'll be left broken

And perpetually terrified of heights

Lost again

Longing for the peace of sandy shores

Leaving pieces of her soul everywhere she goes

Living vicariously through every

Lonely stranger's story

Have you seen that man

He belongs among the stars

He can light up the entire sky with one smile

And put the sun to shame

He is too extraordinary for Earth

(The stars will always welcome him back with open arms)

You call me an angel

But little do you know

I'd gladly rip my wings right off my back

If that meant I could have your heart

And I will never touch his skin

Or run my fingers through his hair

I'll never know how his face changes

Depending on his emotions

I'll never touch him physically

Even though

He has touched me

In ways much deeper

Than fingertips on skin

He found a way to touch my soul

And leave fingerprints

In places where

No one else has reached

(My heart will never be the same)

All the butterflies died

Turns out they can't survive

A broken heart

All the shattered and jagged pieces

Sliced through their beautiful wings

Now I am all left with

Is the bitter taste of your name

And a stomach ache

(Please bring my butterflies back)

With July eyes

And a firework smile

I'd follow you anywhere

As long as you stay for a little while

Make me watch a scary movie with you

I'll lay my head on your chest

And let the steady beat of your heart

Calm the rapid pounding coming from mine

You'll laugh at me

Every time I try and hide my face

Or let out a hushed squeal

I might be scared at the moment

But all the demons and monsters

Lurking in the shadows

Couldn't scare me

As much as the thought of you leaving

I'm all for small talk

But I want to know

Your dreams

I want to know

Your fears

I want to know

Every insignificant thing has ever

Kept you up at night

I want to know every little thought

That runs through your head

But all you're comfortable with

Is small talk

And that's okay

As long as I can hear you talk

Is the flashing red color stained on my lips

From a sweet red wine

Or is it from the blood of the people

Who thought they would break me

Come closer love

Taste for yourself

You have to be a magician

Nothing else can logically explain

How you always tend to disappear

In the blink of an eye

You used my heart as a prop in your act

Putting it in a box

Only to pull out a bouquet of flowers

Instead of returning what was mine

My soul is composed of grains of sand

And you're the tide

Sweeping in and stealing pieces of me

Only to leave again

Never staying for long

Only coming to me

When you have no other choice

(Is it me or the moon calling you back?)

I could take

Every single page

Right from this book

And burn them all

In an attempt to drive you

Out of my words

But I know

I'd still write poems of you

With the ash left on the floor

65079995R00095

Made in the USA
Middletown, DE
01 September 2019